SUCCESS

+

ME

Secret keys to success only smart people know

RUBY BRYANT

TABLE OF CONTENTS

CHAPTER 1 2

The Ability to Delay Gratification....2
Examples of delayed gratification....2
The advantages of delayed gratification....2
Delayed gratification and your career....2
Trust: A crucial aspect in how to delay gratification....2
Ways on How to enhance delayed gratification....2
CHAPTER 2....2
Conscientiousness....2
Characteristics of a Conscientious Person....2
The Subsequent Benefits of Being Conscientious....2
How You Can Become More Conscientious Too....2
CHAPTER 3....2
Socializing with Different Types of People.....2
How to Network for Success....2
How to become successful at networking....2
CHAPTER 4....2
Writing Down Your Goals....2
SMART Goals And How To Use Them For Success....2
How To Make Achievable Goals....2
Why People Fail to Reach Their Smart Goals....2
Self-Evaluation When Setting SMART Goals....2
CHAPTER 5....2
Creating a Powerful Belief System....2
Importance Of Self-Belief....2
Reason Why Some People Lack Self-Belief....2
How To Develop Self-Belief....2
CHAPTER 6....2
Investing In Yourself....2
Various Ways To Invest In Yourself....2
CONCLUSION....2
INTRODUCTION....1

INTRODUCTION

Successful individuals have discovered the appropriate blend of charm, drive, and self-esteem, together with a little bit of luck and excellent timing, while some individuals look like born winners. Most attributes that successful people have may be taught with effort but it starts with recognizing what success means to you.

What Is The Definition Of Success?

How would you define success for yourself? What would you have to accomplish to feel as though you have "made it" in life? When you look at your success, you may prefer to concentrate on just one part of your life, such as your work, your relationships, your money, or if you have accomplished a certain milestone.

However, you will frequently find individuals who look to be prosperous but have suffering relationships, depression, or financial troubles. Perhaps they concentrated so much on one area of achievement that they failed to pay attention to the other vital elements of their life. To achieve overall success in your life, you want to approach your life holistically so that no one pursuit of success adversely affects other elements of your life.

So What is success? Is it wealth? Is it happiness? Is it fame?

Here are several meanings of success.

Not all of them will connect with you, but chances are at least a few of them will. Use these or discover inspiration here to construct your definition of success that can be applied to your unique life.

- **Success means constantly doing your best.**

Success can be reached when you attempt your best in all parts of whatever you do, even if it doesn't lead to significant results.

- **Success is establishing specific objectives.**

Be practical and specific while making objectives. Success does not come from creating abstract objectives. If you know where you're traveling, that is an accomplishment in itself, even if you don't finally reach the intended goal.

- **Success is possessing a place to call home.**

Home is where your heart soars. You are always successful when you can call a location home. Home doesn't have to be a particular building. It might be a nation, a city, or even a person. If you have a location you feel comfortable and protected, you've already accomplished something fantastic.

- **Success is recognizing the difference between necessity and desire.**

If you can meet your monthly responsibilities and satisfy your fundamental necessities, you are successful. Being able to discern when you need something and when you can go without it typically leads to financial stability and is a terrific approach to achieve.

- **Success is believing you can.**

If you think you can, you will succeed. Self-belief doesn't come easy to everyone, so if you're able to persuade yourself that you can reach the objectives in your plans, you're doing fantastic.

When others don't believe in you, you still need to build on your confidence!

- **Success is remembering to mix work with pleasure.**

Work without passion causes needless stress and hollow successes. Focus on what excites you. If you're pleased with your work, that's terrific. However, even if you aren't, you may combine your official career with hobbies or volunteer activities you're enthusiastic about.

- **Success is taking care of your necessities.**

Remember to put on your oxygen mask before aiding others. Self-care is necessary if you wish to make any real effect on the world around you.

- **Success is realizing that you sometimes have to say no.**

Success only comes with a balanced existence. Saying no doesn't mean you are selfish; it just means you have priorities and know what you need to dedicate your focus to at any given moment.

- **Success is knowing your life is filled with wealth.**

Love, health, friends, family, life is filled with plenty. Recognizing this is a vital step to feeling appreciative for what life has provided you. If you can sense this, you are already experiencing success.

- **Success is recognizing you cannot retain what you don't give away.**

You will only succeed if you assist others to succeed. Learning to give instead of constantly taking is part of building a world we all wish to live in. When you help others, you will also create an atmosphere where people desire to help you.

- **Success is conquering fear.**

Conquering fear makes you feel invincible. Even if it's tackling just one tiny fear each week, that is surely something to be pleased of. The biggest phobias may take a longer time, but whatever effort you undertake to conquer fear will lead to success.

- **Success is acquiring something new each day.**

Successful individuals recognize that learning never ends. Take time each day to chat with someone with opposing ideas, and read an intriguing article on a subject you know nothing about. It doesn't take long to learn, so get started immediately.

- **Success is realizing that losing a few battles may help you win a war.**

Successful individuals pick their conflicts intelligently. When you realize which conflicts will eventually help you reach your objectives, you will be successful.

- **Success is caring for others and being loved back.**

Opening your heart to others is challenging and might generate dread. Having the courage to love and receive love from others is a step toward a meaningful life and tremendous achievement.

- **Success is holding your ground when you believe in something.**

Successful individuals never give up on something they believe with all their hearts. You may keep up with views that many people oppose, but if you've done your research and know that it's the right belief for you, you shouldn't let it go without a fight.

- **Success is not giving up.**

Perseverance generates grit, and grit accomplishes accomplishment. Even if it takes years to reach a goal, perseverance is vital if you desire success. When you feel like giving up, reminisce yourself about what you're fighting for. As long as you have a strong "why" you will be able to pursue it.

- **Success is enjoying little triumphs.**

Anytime a goal is attained or obstruction is overcome, take time to celebrate, even if it's something small. All goals need smaller targets to be completed first, so each time you fulfill one, take time to appreciate the effort you put into it.

- **Success is never letting a limitation keep you back.**

Disabilities do not define a person's success. The body and mind will adjust. Just because you can't accomplish absolutely everything doesn't imply you can't do anything. Do what your body and mind allow and constantly push yourself. That is genuine success.

- **Success is recognizing that you control your fate.**

Your destiny is influenced by you and you alone. Take responsibility for your choices and their consequences and you'll discover that you naturally become more successful.

Success may be defined in various ways. If you are enjoying pleasure, love, or adventure now, you've already discovered success. Keep it up.

In this book, we will be looking into some of the secret keys to success only smart individuals know to experience an integrated, satisfying existence.

According to the study, several attributes are crucial for individuals to possess if they want to be successful.

CHAPTER 1

The Ability to Delay Gratification

It feels amazing to have what you desire right at this time. Life is brief, right? But some things that make you feel good or help you escape suffering in the current moment come at the expense of what you desire in your life. These long-term objectives are the incentive for delayed gratification. They don't even have to be that distant in the future but they can offer you greater delight or prevent more serious grief than the promise of the current moment.

Let's take a look at what delayed gratification is, why it's so tough to practice, and how you may get better at it.

What is delayed gratification?

Delayed gratification is the capacity to resist the lure of immediate pleasure. Instead of giving in to temptation, you hold out in the hopes of gaining a greater or longer-lasting future reward.

When you know how to practice delayed gratification, you can wait for what you genuinely desire.

Instant gratification is the reverse of that. Instead of waiting patiently for what you want, you settle for something that will provide you pleasure right immediately.

Examples of delayed gratification

So what does delayed gratification look like? It takes numerous forms depending on the element of life. Let's look at some instances of delayed gratification in personal, professional, and interpersonal aspects:

1. Personal example: good eating habits

Nutrition is a long-term aim that may help you improve your health, regardless of your weight.

But it demands a lot of self-discipline and delayed satisfaction. Indulging in delectable meals that don't adequately feed your body or eating excessive quantities could feel nice at the moment. However, adequate nutrition is a higher prize that takes a long time to obtain. Instead of enjoying fulfillment eating or overeating great but harmful foods all the time, you get to experience the gratification of becoming healthier.

To achieve this, you must be able to sacrifice immediate pleasure and keep your long-term objective of health in mind by having greater impulse control.

2. Professional example: developing yourself for a promotion

Let's imagine you're working for a promotion. To do this, you know you need to learn, improve and strive toward building attributes that constitute a successful leader.

Improving these talents will need you to practice them outside of work, even when you don't always feel like it. It's tempting to cave into quick satisfaction and spend your nights bingeing your favorite TV series. But that won't be rewarding in the long term. Getting the greater prize of promotion instead needs you to spend some time working on yourself. This is so you may become a better leader and boost your chances of attaining your long-term professional objective.

3. Interpersonal example: giving and take

Any healthy relationship has an equal amount of give-and-take from both sides.

When you're creating a connection with someone, your needs can't always come first. Sometimes, you'll need to give so that you may subsequently receive. The consequence is an enduring connection that benefits both sides.

Someone with immediate satisfaction may put their wants first, even when someone they care about needs them. On the other side, delayed gratification helps both partners work together to develop a healthy, equitable relationship.

The advantages of delayed gratification

Delayed gratification is tough. But there are various advantages to not yielding to instant gratification instead.

- **Better Health**

In an experiment, people who were more willing to wait for longer periods were found to have better health in the future. This is likely because they can wait for their satisfaction instead of falling into the lure of bad behaviors.

For example, they'll be better at resisting the impulse to smoke, consume unhealthy foods, skip working out, and drink too much.

- **Improved self-worth**

When you're able to defer your gratification, you can accomplish more of your long-term objectives.

As a consequence, you can show yourself that you're capable of achieving these things. This may help you boost your self-worth.

- **Long-term success**

If you want to attain your long-term objectives, in business and life, you frequently have to make choices. Do I spend my time viewing a movie or completing homework? Do I purchase the new clothing or save the money for a nicer apartment? Doing so frequently delivers a higher return than you would obtain in the short term. When you're able to sacrifice your immediate enjoyment and strive toward your objectives, you may build up success over longer periods.

Delayed gratification and your career

Regardless, if you appreciate your profession, working for a salary demands delayed gratification.

The delayed reward is a paycheck every several weeks.

Over the long run, you may also attain satisfaction via your employment not only obtain a salary but this demands vision. And vision is a crucial fundamental attribute to being a successful leader in business. If you can put in the effort to develop yourself, perform well, and be productive in your organization, you boost your chances of being acknowledged for your devotion.

Keep in mind that deferring satisfaction at work isn't the same as sacrificing everything in your life for your career. It's crucial to maintain a good work-life balance and keep a pulse on your well-being. It simply involves keeping an eye on the longer-term rather than just the current and learning to assess the costs and rewards of each.

Trust: A crucial aspect in how to delay gratification

Delayed gratification cannot exist without first creating trust, particularly in the workplace.

Think about it this way. If you don't believe that your superiors have your best interests at heart, you may struggle with the desire to put in the effort to attain your long-term objectives.

That’s because you may not feel such objectives are possible at all. Delaying gratification becomes less tempting if the future looks unknown and unpredictable.

On the other side, trust offers room for patience and discipline. If you trust that your employer believes in you and will enable you to flourish, you’ll be alright with sacrificing what you want in the near term to create a long-term career instead.

The same approach applies to your personal life. If you don’t trust a buddy, it’ll be tough to make sacrifices for that person.

As a result, you won’t undergo the give-and-take dynamic of a successful relationship because you're unlikely to be keen to give.

If you’re attempting to eat better, you need to believe that it’s doable. Depending on your motive, you need to also think that eating better will give a beneficial benefit to you, prevent sickness, feel more energetic, or lose weight. If you don’t believe that it’s feasible, then resisting the impulse to eat that piece of cake doesn't make very much sense.

Ways on How to enhance delayed gratification

Luckily, you can learn how to delay gratification and get better at it over time. Here are ways to get better at delayed gratification:

- **Understand your values first**

If you don't realize what you're working towards, how can you make sacrifices? That's why it's crucial to identify your work values and personal values before you try to become good at delayed gratification. When you know what you're working towards, it's easier to remember your purpose when you feel tempted.

- **Start with something small**

There's no reason to start stretching your delayed gratification skills with something that's years ahead. Before you work towards your major or long-term ambitions, start with something modest.

The delayed gratification for something little should still be delayed, but it shouldn't need you to wait for too long.

How long you should wait depends on your new ability to achieve delayed gratification. For instance, if you manage to wait one week for a reward, you can start with one day. Over time, you can fabricate the habit into your life.

If there's nothing particular you need to strive for, construct it in your life.

Here's an example. Let's say you want to boost your public speaking skills at work.

The results of your habit won't come right away. However, you can reward yourself for specializing in these skills every day by giving yourself a halt with something fun. This may be viewing one episode of your favorite TV program.

If you don't rehearse, you can't watch, and then you need to wait till tomorrow.

Slowly build up your tolerance over time. Probably you can treat yourself to an outing at the spa after a full month of improving your skills.

- **Use the Seinfeld Strategy**

The Seinfeld Strategy is one of the numerous effective self-satisfaction approaches you may employ to delay gratification for extended periods. Every day that you delay gratification and resist temptation, you cross it off your calendar. After a few days, this produces a chain. This method works nicely for folks who like gamification. If you find it pleasurable to keep the chain running, you're less likely to give in to temptation.

- **Interrupt your autopilot**

Do you discover you are going back to your temptations without thinking about it? If this is the case, you may practice mindfulness to become more conscious of what you do. When you discover you are doing something out of habit, stop for a minute. Ask yourself the reason for doing what you're doing. Take some moment to evaluate how you're feeling. Pay attention to the details.

Take a period of mindfulness to halt your autopilot every time this happens. The more you practice this, the more you'll halt the habit of going for instant gratification.

- **Eliminate temptation**

If you're still trying to delay gratification, discover strategies to reduce the temptation where you can.

For example, let's assume you prefer to spend money on stuff you don't need instead of saving. You might make it tough for yourself to spend that money instead.

Set up automatic payments to a savings account that's tough for you to access. You may even construct this account at a different bank so that you can't quickly transfer the money back.

Start practicing delayed gratification today

Gratification delay is crucial if you want to strive toward long-term objectives. Practicing delayed gratification is just one of the keys you will need to be successful

CHAPTER 2

Conscientiousness

Conscientiousness is a personality quality of being attentive, diligent, thorough, and eager to do what's right.

Conscientious people are extremely structured and accountable in their personal and professional life. Their capacity to plan and manage their impulses has a significant association with achievement.

Studies show that conscientious people have increased rates of job satisfaction, earn higher salaries, and are better at finding jobs and retaining them.

Conscientiousness plays a key part in whether an individual sets and prioritizes long-term goals, values obligations, and makes smart decisions. Those who have these qualities are often very successful due to their hard work and determination. But what about those who don't have this rewarding quality? That's right, this quality is not inherent in all people. And those who weren't born with or taught the power of conscientiousness may be lazy, insensitive, or unreasonable instead.

Characteristics of a Conscientious Person

If the following situations and descriptions resonate with you, it's comfortable to say that you're presumably a very conscientious individual:

If everything around you is not organized, you're not okay.

You keep every single facet of your life organized, from your job to your emails, to your fridge. This allows you to optimize time and also brings a much more stress-free life that allows you to concentrate on what's crucial to you.

You have to get your things done.

One of the primary markers of conscientiousness is one's preoccupation with getting something done and doing it to the best of their ability. So if you're the sort of person who can't even think about sleeping until the laundry's done, the dishes are clean, and you had an overall productive day, then chances are you're a highly conscientious person.

Self-discipline is your middle name.

Are you capable of devoting yourself to attaining a goal? For example, let's imagine that you've signed up for a marathon that takes place in a couple of months. Do you stick to that promise and do all it takes to prepare for the run? People that display self-discipline of the sort are often also exceedingly conscientious.

You provide nothing short of your all.

Not only are you guaranteed to meet your short and long-term objectives, but you ensure that the result is the finest it could be. That shows you put your heart into all you do and are devoted to providing exceptional work.

You think things through.

Conscientious individuals are the last people to accomplish anything on a whim. Instead, they think all of their choices through, they evaluate the advantages and the drawbacks, they comprehend the difference between what they desire and what they need and only then do they act.

You're successful.

It should come as no surprise that conscientious persons are successful, given all of the time they spend planning, creating objectives, working toward their goals, and ensuring they make the proper judgments. If you refuse to accept anything except achievement and victory in life, then you possess the magnificent attribute, that is, conscientiousness.

The Subsequent Benefits of Being Conscientious

There are clear advantages that come with being conscientious, such as the capacity to more easily attain one's objectives owing to self-discipline and dedication. But other advantages are surely worth highlighting as they apply to one's health: according to Harvard Health, conscientiousness is connected most consistently to excellent health. One research indicated that people who were classified as conscientious at an early age by their parents and instructors had longer lives, while another discovered associations between this Big Five personality characteristic and lower blood pressure, reduced likelihood of diabetes and stroke, and fewer joint issues.

Now, why are conscientious folks also healthy ones? Scientists think the explanation is straightforward and obvious: they have superior health practices. People who possess this attribute are less prone to acquire dangerous activities, such as smoking or excessive drinking, and more likely to take to healthy ones. But despite this clear explanation, research is still attempting to determine what particular component of conscientiousness these folks should credit for their good practices.

How You Can Become More Conscientious Too

While some individuals are born conscientious, others have to work at it. If you want to be more conscientious and realize the rewards that come with this characteristic, following these easy tips can help you accomplish so:

- **Start with establishing simple objectives.**

Making tiny objectives and taking little effort will likely lead to more success in adopting the techniques of conscientiousness.

- **Keep yourself accountable.**

Keep a calendar or a planner where you can save track of your goals and plans and keep yourself accountable when you hold to them or don't. You'll be more feasible to stay on track and less prone to make excuses.

- **Focus on what makes you happy.**

People are pleased when they're serving a purpose, donating their efforts to a broader cause, and attaining their objectives. So just recognizing and concentrating on what makes you happy can help you accomplish the ultimate objective of being more conscientious.

- **Eliminate distractions that might get in your way**

If you want to learn how to be diligent, try to get rid of the demon on your shoulder. To achieve this, trim down applications on your phone, declutter your email, and evaluate superfluous and distracting connections. "Having a cleaner living makes it considerably simpler to be organized.

- **Strive to not be emotionally reacting**

Conscientiousness sometimes gets impeded when we're persuaded by an emotional choice. For instance, imagine you're trying to be more conscious about moving on after a split, but every time your ex hits your social media page, your emotions fly into overdrive. In this case, the reasonable thing you can do for yourself and your conscientiousness goals is to stop acting impulsively and reactively.

- **Plan ahead**

Having a plan in place propels being accountable for yourself and your goals much easier and also makes the condition of you flaking on your expectations way less likely. There are many free tools and resources online to plan your days, weeks, and months.

- **Know that learning is a lifelong process**

Learning is not a singular event that just happens. Rather, self-improvement develops progressively over time, drizzled with failures and wins alike. So, just keep in mind that it's a journey, not a destination because this attitude builds conscientiousness

- **Reward yourself for good reinforcement**

Improving a noble personality attribute might involve a lot of effort, so when you accomplish something properly, take notice and recognize it. This attitude of obvious reinforcement is likely to keep your good manners in check and you can even ask other people to participate.

CHAPTER 3

Socializing with Different Types of People.

This is referred to as having an "open network" and is a big predictor of job success. Being exposed to individuals who are different from you and who have various views and opinions helps you to gather knowledge from distinct clusters of people.

It also enables you to be the first to pass on fresh information to other clusters of people and learn how to transfer one group's knowledge into another's insight. These talents help you to detect and take advantage of possibilities that others don't see.

How to Network for Success

Networking provides you success in your life. The better you are at networking, the more successful you'll be in all aspects of your life. Though many factors may stand in the way of becoming an exceptional networker. Some people don't know what to say when they meet someone new and depend on the old stand-bys like the weather.

Maybe you simply don't know the exact strategies essential to network effectively, Here is how

Networking Equals Relationship Building.

If networking is a terrible term for you, you may be thinking about it all wrong. Perhaps you identify networking with attending gatherings where everyone is chatting everyone up and swapping business cards.

You may even imagine networking as the classic "sleazy used car salesmen" image and how much you don't want to look that way. When you think about the necessity to network, you may instinctively place pressure on yourself to succeed. That pressure makes networking seem like a bad thing.

Changing your networking mentality.

If you modify your mentality towards networking, you may start to appreciate the rewards it delivers. You'll have a large number of individuals who know who you are and more chances for yourself than you ever believed conceivable.

Remember, strong leaders know how to network. That's how they got to where they are now. People who make charming small conversations and those with executive presence know how to network.

Increasing your network enhances your net worth.

It's all about relationships. And it's about communicating inside those connections. You can assist others as much as they can help you. Have that Zoom meeting with the person you met. Schedule it for 15 minutes so it's not too considerably of an obligation.

Great networkers are merely terrific communicators.

People who have a broad network usually appear to have an executive presence and a firm and consistent linguistic brand. They get people to like them everywhere they go. They magically formulate their ideas into really well-crafted phrases, and they happen to be wonderful conversationalists. They talk just as effectively to their boss as they do to their closest buddy. They don't succumb to the high risks of reporting to their employer.

Excellent networkers talk clearly and convincingly, of course. And guess what? They weren't born that way. They learned it along the way. They recognized that being an effective and persuasive communicator was in their best interest, so they learned and practiced the essential strategies.

Networking the proper way.

Let's look at networking from a new perspective. What if you regarded it as a properly set out procedure that enabled you to create connections with the individuals you need? When you do that, networking becomes something far better.

Networking properly may be a powerful experience with good outcomes. When you network properly, you'll be in demand, sought after by employers and organizations alike. Just make sure you're communicating clearly.

Look at networking as connection building to modify your perspective towards it. Make it positive. And blow them away with your networking talents.

How to become successful at networking

The necessity of networking is evident. But how can you enhance your networking abilities to guarantee you're networking effectively? When it comes to networking, there are no one-size-fits. Different individuals are successful in utilizing different networking strategies. For instance, if you're an introvert, you may prefer to network one-on-one over coffee or to attend smaller gatherings rather than larger ones. Let's have a look at some alternative tactics for networking.

- **Look for the proper individuals**

Your network career should involve anyone who can help you develop professionally. It may include previous and current co-workers, employers, friends with similar interests, colleagues from business groups, alumni from your institution, or contacts you have met through internet networking sites. Reach out to the individuals who can assist you with the exact aid you need. If you are interested in working in a different sector, connect with friends or family members who work in that area. You never know who may be able to assist you at a later point, so be sure to connect with individuals working in a range of businesses and professions.

- **Be proactive**

Cultivating your network year-round is vital to sustaining valuable ties. Don't only call those who can assist after you have recently been laid off from your work or decide you want to hunt for new employment. Maintain contacts with your extended network at all times, even only by sending a simple email to say hello. The stronger your ties are with your contacts, the more ready they will be to offer a hand and support you when you are in need. People are more eager to assist when they know who you are.

- **Keep track of your network**

Keep track of your career network someplace. Whether it's online or on paper, be sure you know who is who, where they work, and how to get in contact. It is crucial to keep track of what the various connections in your network can provide you or how you might assist them. You will need to recall which of your past employees currently works in finance or which began teaching philosophy. Equally crucial is to know what you have to offer as a contact. Ideally, networking should be mutually beneficial, so be sure to let your network know how you can assist them. If you are prepared to encourage your pals, they are more likely to return the favor.

- **Attend networking events**

Networking in person works. Attending workplace mixers, corporate getaways or community gatherings will expose you to a range of crucial connections. Possibly others at the events will also be networking and will be glad to exchange business cards or contact information. There are many various sorts of networking events you may attend that happen year-round, both in person and electronically.

- **Network online**

Especially in today's society, it might be tough to network in person, but technology has made networking online easier. The internet is a fantastic resource for generating, nurturing, and connecting with your connections. Sites like LinkedIn and Facebook may assist you to get in contact with individuals at certain organizations, with other college grads, or in a specified geographic region. Sending a friend request or a quick note to a new contact may help them remember you and urge them to seek out a mutual connection. Always make sure your web presence is up-to-date since even recruiters utilize professional networking sites and certain social media channels to analyze abilities and expertise. If you don't have an internet presence, start establishing one as soon as possible, since it will help you in the future.

These tips will improve your networking success. A reliable network can bring in new clients, potential partners, business and career opportunities, and seasoned mentors. It's never too late or too early to invest in your network. The greatest method to develop your networking abilities is to put yourself out there and give it a shot.

Take the time to locate the perfect sort of networking approach for you and concentrate on making it a fantastic experience.

CHAPTER 4

Writing Down Your Goals

The first thing you do in the morning will establish what your day is going to be like. Program your mind to be in a strong condition from the time of awakening, and you are certain to have a productive and excellent day.

How you can achieve this, is by writing your goals down, every morning. Then, after you've done that, circle the most significant goal, the one that in the long-term will have the largest influence on your life.
Now ask yourself this question: "What actions can I take today that will change everything and propel me closer to my goal?" Write down all the acts you can think of, circle the two most crucial ones and start

performing them. Don't stop till it's done. This is a very strong approach to being in the correct state first thing in the morning. Instead of meandering about half-dead and spending 30 minutes to wake up, you are hacking your mind to be productive.

Another significant reason for writing down your goals is that reading them helps us feel good, write them as if they're already attained. You're already there.

Re-reading and re-writing them every morning will enable you to be in a resourceful mindset where you act depending on your objectives. You will make purposeful choices throughout the day that will support your objectives and lead you closer to them.

Goals that are not noted are just wishes

SMART Goals And How To Use Them For Success

The cornerstone of all successfully realized goals is the SMART goal. But what is it?

SMART is an abbreviation for

Specific,

Measurable,
Attainable,
Relevant, and
Time-based.

It has been utilized by organizations and people to attain their aims and objectives and is a formula that, on the whole, works effectively.

The strength of SMART goals is that they provide a clear route to accomplishing goals, and they have a defined time in which to achieve them.

Let's look at the wise goal-setting criterion

Specific

For a goal to be feasible, it has to have a very clear result. The clearer the aim, the more likely it is you will attain it.

For example, if you only state "I want to lose weight," then theoretically you could fulfill your objective just by not eating supper for one week, you would lose weight that way, even if it were temporary.

You need to have a more precise goal: "I want to drop thirty pounds by the end of this year."

Measurable

To accomplish anything, it's necessary to have quantifiable objectives. Take the example above: "I want to shed some fats by the end of this year."

It's quantifiable since all you need do is weigh yourself at the beginning of your trip, then subtract thirty pounds from that. Set your new weight goal for December 31, then each week weigh yourself to monitor progress.

Attainable

What makes a goal attainable? Being attainable indicates that SMART goals are feasible and that you have everything you need to accomplish them.

In our scenario of reducing weight, 30 pounds in six months is entirely achievable. Your resources may include a gym membership, some at-home, or inspiration to go outdoors and run every day.

Relevant

For any goal to be realized, you need to define appropriate goals for your individual life. If reducing weight is achievable, given the lifestyle you live, and if you feel it will lead to a better, healthier life, then it is surely relevant to you. It's much more significant if your doctor has pointed out that you need to reduce weight to avert health risks.

Time-based

Finally, you need a timeframe. All your goals need to have an end date since it provides a feeling of urgency and gives you a deadline.

In our example of losing thirty pounds, a timetable of six months would be particular, quantifiable, relevant, and would have a deadline. Furthermore, since you have everything you need to reach that objective, it is feasible

How To Make Achievable Goals

The difficulty always found with the SMART goal formula is that it does not take into consideration the human component. We need motivation and a cause for reaching our objectives.

For example, if you intend to lose thirty pounds, you are going to spend several months feeling hungry, and unless you possess superhuman mental power, you are going to give in to the food cravings.

All SMART goals may be reduced down to three words:

What do you want to achieve?

Why do you want to accomplish it?

How are you going to accomplish it?

When you simplify your aim in this manner, accomplishing it becomes a lot simpler. Here are some ways to make your goals achievable

Visualize What You Want

One technique to make your objectives feasible is to imagine the eventual outcome. When you put up your mission statement, you should be visualizing what it would be like after you have accomplished the objective.

In our weight loss scenario, you would shut your eyes and visualize the process till December

Identify Your "Why"

The more remarkable your goals, the better.

Your why may be. If your why is, "Since my doctor instructed me to lose some weight," that is not a good "why" because it's your doctor's, not yours.

One technique to establish your "why" is to compose your mission statement.

To assist in setting feasible SMART goals, complete the following mission statement:

" *STATE your GOAL CLEARLY by writing the dATE YOU WANT TO COMPLETE THE GOAL" because of your Why*

If you wish to create a SMART goal using the weight loss example, your mission statement would be written: "I will lose thirty pounds by the end of this year because I want to look and feel amazing in December"

Never draft a mission statement that is full of unclear terms. The language you employ should be basic, direct, and unambiguous.

Figure Out Your, "How"

Before you can begin to reach your goal, you need to construct a list of measures you can do to make it happen. Write down anything you can think of that will help reach your goal. It doesn't matter what order you put these activities down, what matters is that you write down as many action steps as you can think of. Always aim for roughly one hundred modest steps. This makes it much simpler to assign activities for each day that not only bring you ahead on your goal but also keep you engaged every day in reaching it.

Once you have your list, you may build a to-do list for the goal and assign the tasks to various days so you generate momentum towards a good end.

Patience

Without patience, you will give up. To accomplish anything good demands patience. Success does not happen overnight. Be patient and enjoy the process of moving a bit closer to accomplishing your goals each day.

Action

If you do not take action on any goal, then even SMART goals won't be reached. You need to make sure you remind yourself of your goals and why you want to attain them each day. Read your goal statement, establish an action plan, and then take the appropriate steps to make sure you get a step closer each day.

Consistency

The activity you do each day towards accomplishing your goal has to be consistent. You can't follow your eating regimen for a week and then take three weeks off. It doesn't work that way, you have to be consistent to accomplish your aim. A saying goes that
"Success is a few easy disciplines performed every day."

Time

Of course, you need to provide adequate time between where you are now and where you want to be in the future. Be realistic about time, and don't become upset if you miss your deadline. Re-adjust your timeline if required.

Why People Fail to Reach Their Smart Goals

Setting SMART goals and attaining them is not easy, and many people fail.

The difficulty is that many individuals regard goals as hopes and desires. They think they will lose some weight, they aspire to start their own company, or they have a desire to acquire a better job. The issue with “hoping” and “wishing” for anything is that there is no strategy, no purpose, and no period defined for reaching the objectives.

Once these dreams and desires meet face-to-face with the reality of everyday life, they swiftly evaporate into lost hopes and wishful thinking. Therefore, to genuinely accomplish anything, you need a precise aim: a SMART goal.

Self-Evaluation When Setting SMART Goals

Despite knowing what SMART goals are and how to successfully write them down, some people will succeed in setting their goals while others will fail.

That is the nature of goals. Despite your greatest efforts, occasionally you’ll come up short. But that’s alright since this illustrates another facet of goals.

You know, goals evolve in so many ways, and they may change, too. As you go through your goals, you could make revisions to them.

Maybe you need a bit more time, or you weren't anticipating other life distractions to dig into your time. Regardless, this is how you want to approach and analyze these aspects:

Evaluating Failure

Take failure as a learning opportunity. It's an opportunity for you to learn about yourself and your goal-setting tactics. From there, you may take that knowledge and begin to make improvements before trying the objective again.

It is crucial that if you have hurdles or setbacks, you don't accept them as such. These are difficulties and chances for development and further modification. The aim is to walk away from these characteristics with greater information than before.

Evaluating Success

While this is a terrific moment to savor your achievements, you should also utilize this opportunity for introspection, possibly even more than with failure.

Success is amazing, but that frequently leads to the question of "what's next?" And for most people, this is not a simple question to answer. All in all, prosperity might lead to us stagnating, which is bad. That's not to imply that we need to be continually attaining and creating goals. You should surely be celebrating successes large or small.

Nevertheless, there comes a level where we need to analyze that success. What have you gained from that success? What can you do to keep moving forward to achieve more? What do you want to do next?

By asking deeper questions about what you have done, you may further improve yourself and narrow down what needs to be focused on next.

Whether it's individual or business goals, when you have a strong personal "why" for your goal, your inspiration to keep going stays strong.

Start with your "why," and then get started on the action steps that will carry you to the conclusion.

CHAPTER 5

Creating a Powerful Belief System

Ask any successful individual what their number one rule for succeeding is. They all have something in common: They believe in themselves and what they're doing, and they are not afraid to tell it. If you don't acknowledge yourself, why would anybody else?

When others question you about your ambitions in life, don't be scared to speak it out loud. If you have lofty objectives, people could scoff and look at you weird. But if you're uncertain about your ambitions, you will make insecure choices that will bring you nowhere.

Go against the grain, and stand out, after all, how many individuals in the world today are genuinely living their dreams? Now, how many of these folks would say something along the lines of "I don't know" if you inquire what their aims are?

Be determined and trust in yourself. People will appreciate you for having the bravery for going for what you want.

The first step to living and attaining your goal is to believe it and picture it. When you think in your mind that you've already attained your objectives, you will create a feeling of assurance. That clarity will lead to action steps, because you know what the conclusion is going to be it's much simpler to pick out the measures that are essential to get there.

By continually repeating in your mind the ideas of your achievement, you develop neural connections in your brain. Your mind can't detect the difference between what you vividly envisage and the truth.

Go out and daydream. Go forth and believe, picture already realizing your desires and objectives. With enough repetition, you feel confident that this is the only consequence and you work to discover strategies for making it happen.

Importance Of Self-Belief

As the name indicates, self-belief has to do with how much a person believes in him or herself. It includes the belief in your ideals, talents, expertise, and abilities. Self-believe is incredibly significant since it impacts a person's lifestyle and decisions.

A person lacking self-belief would consistently underestimate their ability while settling for less than what they deserve. Most times, the person accepts whatever hit life throws because they do not think that they deserve more.

On the other hand, a person with self-belief realizes their worth and value.

For instance, when individuals with low self-belief find a job opening with the talents they possess, they may pass up on it or apply half-heartedly because they feel that they are not competent enough for the position.

People with self-belief, on the other hand, would seek the job totally because they think that they are well-qualified for the position.

In the end, persons without self-belief may end up doing a poor-paying job and living at the mercy of others for the rest of their life. Meanwhile, persons with self-belief will go from that position to a better one and could finally reach the apex of their professions.

This example indicates that although self-belief can appear minor or trivial, it can affect our whole life both directly and indirectly.

Self-belief inspires individuals to explore their potential and this motivation may lead to the realization of goals.

Reason Why Some People Lack Self-Belief

No one is born without self-belief. Most times, we find ourselves in particular events and circumstances that might adversely influence our self-esteem either momentarily or in the long term.

To recover your self-belief, recognizing the event that caused you to lose it might help you discover how to continue.

Here are some prevalent reasons for lack of self-belief:

- **Unhappy Homes**

Growing up in an unhappy family might impair a person's conviction in themself. This is because as youngsters, the way you are treated by others, particularly by your family, greatly shapes the way you regard yourself.

Kids who grow up with parents who never applaud or congratulate them (but grumble and tear them down) grow up without confidence in themselves.

- **Negative Peers**

Being surrounded by individuals who consistently discourage you and make you feel like you are not good enough might make you lose confidence in yourself. Sometimes, your peers may even encourage you to do things you are not comfortable with and when you reject them, they may say and do things to make you feel uncomfortable. To fit in, you may find yourself discarding your ideals and beliefs to suit others.

- **Traumatic Experiences**

Physical and mental abuse may break down a person's self-belief. If you have a spouse that makes you feel like you are not good enough to attract and hold their attention, it may extend to you feeling like you are not decent enough for anyone Also, persons who encounter physical abuse may suffer from sadness and anxiety, which may progressively erode their self-esteem. Eventually, such an event will make them feel undeserving of their aspirations.

- **Bad Decisions**

Some bad decisions compelled in the past can influence a person's belief in him or herself and cause them to dispute their ability to make decisions in the future. This generally occurs when the choice taken turns out to have implications that touch not only the individual but also their loved ones.

- **Negative Thought**

If you continuously think about the worst-case possibilities, particularly when it comes to yourself, chances are that you will lose confidence in yourself.

If before a job interview, the only thing you can think about is all the errors you could make or how you might not be as excellent as other applicants, you will probably take in that energy and discourage your interviewers. Over time, such negative thinking patterns could cause you to feel unworthy and inferior to everyone else. That is why you need to think positively and reject negative ideas.

How To Develop Self-Belief

Once you understand the cause of your lack of self-belief, you may continue to work on how to develop it.
Here are ways to help you develop your self-belief.

- **Know Who You Want to Be**

When self-doubt or self-pity is not gnawing at you, who would you want to be? If you were not frightened, what would you do?
Boldly addressing these questions is the first step to regaining your self-belief. This is because the doubts and negative thinking

patterns, over time, bury the real you along with your objectives and aspirations.

To increase self-belief, you need to strive towards these objectives while pushing away poor self-esteem. So, allow yourself the freedom to dream a bit, and write a list of all the things you would want to accomplish and believe. While doing this, anytime self-doubts pop up, push them aside until you produce a full list.

- **Affirm Yourself**

Self-affirmations are great tools that encourage your conviction in yourself. This is because as humans, our self-image drives our conduct. If you consider yourself as one of the most good-looking persons in the world, you will undoubtedly act like one and if you perceive yourself as the future CEO of a corporation, you will also behave like one. So, what you need to do is consider yourself as someone deserving and great.

Affirmations may assist you to build that picture. There are positive affirmations that wipe off doubts, particularly when uttered loudly and with conviction.

For example:

" I am capable of everything I desire." "I am smart enough to accomplish my goals." "I am privileged to all the greatest things life has to offer." "And I will put out effort every day to attain one particular desire and one precise aim to appreciate the finest things."

So compose a list of affirmations, stand in front of your mirror and speak these things to yourself. It does not have to be long. Just four inspirational statements may make you feel prepared to confront the world each day.

- **Face Your Fears**

One effective technique to increase self-belief is through addressing your anxieties. You may opt to start little by little. Start by unraveling the source of your self-doubt and tackling that problem. If your parent's treatment of you as a youngster is the reason you lost confidence in yourself, contact them and talk to them about it.

Next, deal with the fear of failing to attain your goals. Address that board of directors with your beliefs and creations. Walk out of that relationship that consistently beats on your self-esteem.

- **Address Your Inner Critic**

If society is the cause for your lack of self-belief, it may simply be addressed and repaired. If you are your critic, though, your confidence cannot be rebuilt if you do not shut off the condemning voice in your brain. Most often, the lack of conviction in oneself is a consequence of excessive inner criticism. You can have this wonderful concept but when preparing the proposal, you may start thinking about whether the idea is good enough. You then start to persuade yourself that the plan is not good enough, tossing the piece of paper, and putting the idea behind the lock and key.

Addressing your inner critic is vital because until you do, you may keep diminishing your skills and settle for less than you deserve and then go on to spell out all the reasons why you are qualified for the role. Doing this continually will shut your inner critic up and build your self-belief tremendously.

- **Be Prepared to Win**

Before you take a step towards your goals and dreams, be sure you are fully set up to win. Do not do things on a whim or have a 'winging it' approach since they generally fail. Instead, study hard for that test, prepare to deliver all the best answers at that interview, produce an amazing presentation for that meeting, and cut off acquaintances who pollute your head with negative ideas.

Preparing to win also inspires you with confidence that will drive you to put in the additional effort to attain your purposes in life.

- **Encourage Others**

Do you realize that supporting others may transform your thinking about success? Most times, a lack of self-belief may also lead to losing trust in other people's skills. You can find yourself continuously advising individuals against going for their aspirations because you doubt that they can attain them. So make an effort to perceive success as something everybody can accomplish.

Encourage your friends and family, and your mentality about success will also shift over time. Soon your encouragement will shift inwards, and you will start feeling inspired to attain your objectives.

- **Take Care of Yourself**

To improve your self-belief, you need to take care of yourself and not only psychologically and emotionally. Physical care may go a long way toward impacting your mental and emotional wellbeing.

So, go to a spa and have a massage. Go shopping for garments that make you feel nice and do your hair. Register at the gym, eat properly, and make sure you get adequate rest. Also, speak to a therapist or join a support group.

Looking nice and feeling good can undoubtedly assist enhance your self-confidence.

- **Cut Off Negative Acquaintances**

So-called friends who make you feel inadequate or not good enough with their words or behavior should be cut off. This is because having such individuals around you would undermine every attempt you make to repair your self-esteem. If your family are the ones treating you wrongly, talk to them about it, and make it evident that you will not condone negativity in your life. If your relationship is physically or emotionally abusive, cut the individual off too clear, until you do, your self-belief may never increase.

While removing yourself from unpleasant acquaintances, bring your cherished friends and family closer and create good ties.

Be yourself, being someone else is a waste of who you are

So, if the reason you lost your self-belief is that you believe others are better than you, you need to make a knowledgeable effort into changing that mindset. Think of all the remarkable things you can do that other people cannot. And remember that you are just as deserving as the next person.

CHAPTER 6

Investing In Yourself

A wise man was once asked what the best possible investment a person could make was, invest in yourself." he said.

Hiring a personal coach, getting a membership at a gym, and buying healthy foods, books and education are not expenses. They are investments, investments in yourself.

Various Ways To Invest In Yourself

- **Exercising**

Exercise releases endorphins and makes you feel great. It improves productivity and energy levels. By investing time in the gym, you'll be adequately able to handle daily tasks and what life tosses at you. Getting enough exercise every day is one of the best ways to invest in yourself

Exercise can also be done by walking, dancing, hiking, swimming, etc exercise. It doesn't matter what type of exercise you do, in as much as it's something you enjoy and can do most days.

- **Eating good food.**

When you go to the grocery store after work, ask yourself to eat foods that will nourish your mind and body and will make you feel and perform better by doing this You are setting yourself up for success by consciously making yourself aware of what foods will empower you, therefore making better decisions.

- **Reading books.**

Everyone buys books, but very few read them cover to cover. Stop reading books and start studying them. only a Few people read the books they buy, but even fewer remember what they read.

Studying at least an hour a day will make you succeed in your chosen career

- **Daily Journaling**

Keeping a daily journal might sound like an incredible way to invest in yourself. daily journaling can make you more self-reflective, and this can be an important element of success. Writing out your thoughts and feelings allows you to release them in a safe, nonjudgmental space.

- **Doing something for yourself.**

Yes, hard work is a major factor in succeeding, but at least once per month do something fun, something outrageous and spontaneous that makes you feel alive. Have fun and enjoy yourself.

- **Strengthening Your Current Skills**

No matter what you do, you already have and use an expansive range of skills in your career and your life but are you regarded as an "expert" in the skills or areas you rely on most? Probably not.

Improving the skills you rely on is one of the best ways to invest in yourself since you already have basic knowledge in at least one particular area. It's far more reasonable to become an expert in a field you're already familiar with than one that you know nothing about.

- **Learning a New Skill**

Learning a new skill not only keeps your mind sharp, but also adds yet another tool you can use to perform better in your career, qualify for a promotion, or even start your own business. Think about a new skill that would enable you to succeed in your current day job or a career you will like to focus on in the future.

Learning public speaking skills can make you a more effective presenter when you're pitching ideas to your boss or prospective clients.

Strengthening your finance skills can help you save extra money to start a business or side gig.

Taking the time to learn a new language can help you land a new job or achieve promotion.

- **Attending Seminars and Workshops**

Seminars, conferences, and workshops are excellent alternatives for investing in yourself. These events help broaden your knowledge in an area or field you're knowledgeable about. Improving your knowledge and skills can help you build expert status and make you more productive in your current role.

They're also great networking opportunities for meeting professionals in your industry and making great connections with other like-minded people or finding a mentor who can help you in your career.

- **Breaking Your Bad Habits**

We all have poor habits. Some of us don't get enough exercise, while others consume too much fast food or prefer to delay. You could gnaw your nails, spend too much time watching Netflix, watch too much TV, or worry over your issues at night. Only you know what your terrible habits are. They're the bad behavior patterns that impair your physical, emotional, or social well-being. And if you're like most people, you have a lengthy list of habits you'd want to cease doing.

Making an effort to stop your bad habits can be immensely freeing, and when you replace a poor habit with a good one such as exercising frequently or getting enough sleep, it may improve your life.

Breaking a bad habit requires work and effort. It also helps to have a plan.

- **Find a Creative Outlet**

According to research from LinkedIn Learning, creativity was the ability that everyone sought in 2020. This was the second year creativity earned the top rank, so it will probably continue to be in high demand in the years to come.

Many individuals believe they're not creative because they can't sketch a picture or create a piece of music. However, that's a limiting way to look at creativity. Humans are, by nature, creative creatures. Everyone, including you, is creative in some manner.

Some creative financial planners come up with unique and fresh methods for their customers to save money or develop a retirement nest egg, creative sales professionals discover new and interesting ways to deliver outstanding presentations, and creative real estate investors find new ways to invest. Parents depend on creative thinking all the time, watch any parent stop a screaming 3-year-old in the grocery store without resorting to sugar.

At its core, creativity is about solving issues or offering people a fresh way to look at an old or established notion. Learning how to be more creative can boost your reputation at work and bring more success and joy into your life.

You can learn how to access your creativity just as you can acquire any other ability. Start by compiling a list of any creative projects or hobbies you've always wanted to try. It might help to start with executing some tiny creative work without pausing to judge or edit what's on the page, such as sketching with your eyes closed or fast writing about whatever comes to your mind.

Investing in yourself involves creating modest, constant changes that allow you to do more, be more, grow more, and love more.

These minor adjustments may lead to instant opportunity and long-term beneficial change. They may help you make more money or start working from home, find the profession you always wanted, pursue your ambitions, and explore hobbies that fill you with delight. They'll enhance your health and relationships, make you a more fascinating person, and lead to a better life.

CONCLUSION

One of the greatest temptations in the current culture is to fall into the trap of being on autopilot, to be walking dead and do what everyone else is doing. Most of us are too busy reacting and responding to the environment and what's occurring around us.

While we should act and take responsibility for our universe and our reality. We neglect to keep focused and we forget about our aims. Learn to be mindful. Being more mindful of your day-to-day choices will lead you to take the proper activities to attain success.

Have a purpose in life, live according to your principles, and don't allow anyone to tell you what to do or how things should be. When you start to make more conscious choices, you will start to think about whether this is going to lead you closer to success or drift you farther away.

If you genuinely want to follow your objectives and see them come true, you need to start taking steps mindfully. In the end, you have to find out what success means for you in all aspects of your life.

The final piece of advice and rule to follow is to "Keep on"

Sometimes, things become rough and the path feels too long. You simply have to keep on, staying on.

Revisit your objectives and start visualizing, all of a sudden you've transformed your state and you're on the correct route again.

Use these keys to construct your destiny and get what you desire in life.

www.ingramcontent.com/pod-product-compliance
Lightning Source LLC
LaVergne TN
LVHW052030170826
845678LV00018B/2503